The CAREGIVER CHRONICLES

*Tales of Encouragement and
Hope for Caregivers, Family, and Friends*

PHIL LEICHLITER

ISBN 979-8-88943-544-0 (paperback)
ISBN 979-8-88943-545-7 (digital)

Christian Faith Publishing
832 Park Avenue
Meadville, PA 16335
www.christianfaithpublishing.com

Printed in the United States of America

To all of the wonderful caregivers who bless and help others.

Foreword

This is a special book. Phil Leichliter cared lovingly for his wife, Diana, for over two decades. He devoted himself to her comfort and safety and enjoyment of life. He describes in his ode to Diana, her grace and her faith, as well as her progressive symptoms of Huntington's disease (HD), a cruel neurodegenerative disorder for which there is not yet truly effective treatment or a cure. As a genetic counselor at UCSF for thirty-four years and the creator of the UCSF HD clinic, I had the privilege of knowing families over many years, observing the physical, behavioral, cognitive, and emotional progression in the affected individuals, as well as the unavoidable impact on their family members. I met with Phil and Diana over several years and was always struck by their love and resilience and their faith. Now, four years following Diana's demise, Phil's book is a truly authentic, brutally honest personal story of kindness and faith. Phil describes his own experiential path and offers a myriad of useful, creative ideas for giving care while walking side by side with God. It is a book filled with truth; Diana was a blessing and a joy giver. It is a book about everlasting love.

Phil takes you by the hand and shares with you his love and gratitude. His book helps you prepare for moments of joy and of pain, the nuance of the simplest suggestions and the most meaningful responses, allowing you to provide compassionate care. Savor this book. Your heart will open.

—Andrea Zanko, MS, genetic counselor, University of California–San Francisco, Genetics Clinic (retired); creator of the UCSF Huntington's Disease Clinic

Unresponsive—that is the last word anyone would ever want to have to say or hear regarding their loved one. I remember my father telling me about how he had to load my mother into the car and drive her to the hospital. He carried her inside and simply shouted *"unresponsive"* to the emergency room attendants. The word must have felt like it weighed a thousand pounds. As the hospital staff took his wife from his arms, I am sure he still felt the weight. The weight of a loss he had known was inevitable, one that he had fought against and dreaded for years. I have watched my dad take care of her my entire life, and I have never seen anyone give so much and stand by their vow to another person with that level of dedication. He is truly the greatest man I will ever know. So as you read this book, I hope it helps you. They are stories about sacrifice, of success, and failure, but in the end, it is ultimately a love story.

—Caleb D. Leichliter, son of Diana and Phil Leichliter

Introduction

We take so much for granted in our day-to-day lives. We flip the light switch, and the light comes on. We turn the key or press the button, and our car engine roars to life. We stand up, and we can walk across the room without falling. We breath in and out and swallow our food without thinking a thing about it.

Sometimes, however, things don't go just as we thought they would. Sometimes you might notice that the flirty, beautiful young woman you married and planned to grow old with has begun to show signs that something is…wrong, or your dad, who was always strong and articulate, has begun to fade into Alzheimer's, or the man you married can no longer remember how to put on his socks.

Everyone *intends* to be noble, to be kind and caring, but time, fatigue, and loneliness can begin to erode our resolve. There can be times of hopelessness and discouragement. Our well-meaning friends sometimes say innocent but hurtful things. And then perhaps you get yet *more* bad news from the doctor.

The *good news* is that you are not alone!

Chapter 1

Facing Fear

On June 12, 1995, the waiting room at the neurology center at the University of California–San Francisco was cold, the air conditioner seemingly set at refrigerator-like temperature. Our conversation had a slight chill as well, making only small talk, avoiding the elephant in the room. Looking around, there were individuals, mostly with care-givers, who had obvious neurological disorders. I noticed my wife, Diana, looking at one, then the next, and I could tell what she was thinking, *Lord, is that my future?*

We knew for more than ten years that something was terribly wrong, but the medical community could only guess; there was no actual test to determine the existence of the Huntington gene in a patient…so they had to rely on symptoms to guess that it must be HD (Huntington's disease). They would basically try to rule out other illnesses by the process of elimination. And then based on the symptoms and their experience, they would say, "We believe it's Huntington's disease."

Diana exhibited such grace and strength as she took the newly developed genetic test. She knew in her heart, even before agreeing to do the testing, that the result would be positive for the HD gene in her DNA, but somehow that did not reduce the anxiousness in her spirit. It took a week for the results to come in, and our return appointment was actually the start of a new chapter in our lives. We determined together to face the fear and live an overcoming life.

Little did we know how hard it would be to live up to those hopeful, lofty aspirations!

As we were leaving, Diana said, "What do people *do* who don't know the Lord?" Then she said, almost as a new motto, "God's grace is sufficient."

Something to think about:

When suddenly you find that your world is changing, and you feel helpless, as though being swept along by an ocean wave, what do you cling to? What's your first reaction? Maybe the doctor will give you sedatives? Maybe a couple of glasses of wine every evening? Perhaps a relationship with someone that you know you should not have? Sorry, but these are *not* things that will actually help; in fact, it's well documented that most of these things add difficulty and complications to your life. Did you know that it is possible to have *true joy* even when you're unhappy? It's true! Joy and happiness are not the same thing! Now is the time to really think about the *true* joy giver.

Let's pray:

Lord, I pray that you will make yourself very *real* to the reader right now. Wash over them with your peace, your joy, and touch their heart! Cause the reader to reach out to you in the most basic of ways. Let them cling to you, to cry on your mighty chest! Stand with them, and be their strong tower! *Amen*!

> The name of the Lord is a strong tower; God's people run to it, and are safe! (Prov. 18:10)

Chapter 2

The New Normal

When you're caring for someone who is affected by a disease that is long-term and has a slow progression, sometimes you are too close to the situation to even see the gradual changes that are taking place. With Huntington's disease, both slow and rapid changes are possible, and there's simply no way to predict how things will be a year or even a month from today. I have had many occasions where a friend or loved one, who has not been with us for a few months, stands speechless for a few moments when seeing Diana again, and then whispers to me, "Wow, there's been a lot of change since last time I saw her." After a while, I was no longer bothered by those types of comments because they are simply a natural response to the cruel progression of the disease.

Sometimes, however, there are milestones. Some are bittersweet milestones, like the date I realized Diana had lived longer than her mother, who died of the same cruel disease. Another was the date that Diana became old enough to apply for Social Security benefits, with an early retirement at age sixty-two. Then there are the big, life-changing milestones. In a number of instances, it's something that makes a very positive change for us but nonetheless were challenging when we faced them. One example was the whole routine of feeding Diana. It had become more and more challenging because of her increasing difficulty with swallowing. Almost every mealtime, Diana would choke, sometimes badly! This caused her so much distress and made mealtimes so hard! We finally decided to have a G-tube (feeding tube) inserted so that Diana could receive nourishment with almost no risk of choking. I remember thinking to myself, *Well, Phil, you keep picking up new life skills that you never thought you would need.*

Something to think about:

Sometimes we wish we knew the future. I'm so glad we *don't*! I'm confident that if we knew all the things that life would throw at us over the course of time, we could not endure. Ten years prior, if someone would have told me what my daily routine ten years later would involve, it could have been so discouraging! But because I'd taken on each "new normal" situation a little at a time, God gave me the grace and strength to deal with them. Remember, the things that happen to you may have been a surprise to *you*, but they were *not* a surprise to God. That's why it's so important to keep your focus on *him*, and don't allow hardships, fatigue, financial challenges, or anything to cause you to stop "resting in him." His Word says, "You will keep him in perfect peace whose minds are steadfast, because they trust in you. Trust in the Lord forever, for the Lord, the Lord himself is the Rock eternal" (Isaiah 26:3).

Let's pray:

Heavenly Father, I ask that you give the reader *peace* right now, that you will make yourself very real to them. Help them to learn to really know you as the joy giver for their life! Draw them to you, Father. Show them your love, your care, and let them know that you know how to care for what belongs to you! Lord, in your Word, you've made it clear that when we are feeling weak, *you* are best able to demonstrate your strength and power (2 Corinthians 12: 8–10). Amen!

Chapter 3

Changing Relationships— Family Friends

Diana and I had a nice circle of friends for many years, going to dinner together, kids in school together, church activities. And when Diana was diagnosed with the disease, they pledged their never-ending support. They said they cared and said, "Please just let us know how we can help!" Over time however, I noticed that some of them were growing a little distant. I couldn't put my finger on it exactly, but clearly, something had changed in the relationship. I didn't think much of it because my life was so full and so busy, but soon I started to realize that our circle was growing smaller. Couples we used to speak with regularly seem to be "really busy" lately or unavailable when you ask if they are interested in going out to dinner. The friends at church who used to sit with us still sit near us, but there is no familiar banter before the service starts, and afterward they slip away before I can chat with them.

Finally, I decided to confront one of my friends that used to be pretty close and ask them what's happened. My friend looks at me with a helpless look on her face and finally blurts out, "I just don't know what to say! Your wife has changed so much, and I just don't know what to say to her. And I'm scared!"

Something to think about:

What you're experiencing is so very normal and common. Sadly, most people simply don't know how to interact with people who have disabilities or grave illnesses. They think they have to have the right words to say. And because of that, sometimes they say things like "Don't worry, God will make a way" or "I'll keep you in my prayers" or "Hang in there! Be strong." Please know, they honestly don't realize that *all they truly need to do* is be there for you. They need to come and sit with you quietly and listen. They need to come sit with you and pray. They need to offer to pick up groceries for you. What *you* need to do is realize they *truly want* to help, but they honestly don't know the words to say or the things to do so *ask them.* Say, "I could really use some help with grocery shopping," or "Would you please come sit and have a cup of coffee with me?" and you'll be surprised at how quickly they will truly delight in doing something tangible to help you.

Let's pray:

Father, please give me a holy boldness to ask our friends for the kind of help that we need. Give us strength for the day and wisdom to deal with well-meaning people who are simply unequipped to interact with those who are disabled or ill. Give me patience to love them with the same love you have demonstrated to *me*, Father! You see me with all my faults and shortcomings, yet somehow you still love me and want to have a relationship with me! Thank you for walking through these difficulties with me, Lord! *Amen!*

Chapter 4

Is There Anyone to Help?

Finally, you start to recognize that the care needs of your loved one are growing to the extent that you alone might not be able to handle them by yourself. You have a full-time job, trying to keep the bills paid, and you rush home to care for your loved one right after work and sometimes find that they've fallen or could not reach the drink of water they needed, and you feel you're failing more and more each day. You ask some family members if they can help, but they are not available at the times that you really need help! You start checking with the agencies and with online services, and *wow,* you didn't realize they were so expensive! You try for disability with Medicare, but they somehow say your loved one does not qualify, or even if they *do* qualify, the help that's available simply isn't the kind of help you actually need. Some well-meaning friends tell you that maybe you should "put them in a home" or even divorce so that you won't be burdened with the cost of care that you simply cannot afford. You truly begin to feel helpless, like you're drowning. But don't despair! The *very best* helpers available might not even have experience or training for caregiving. What you really need is someone that has a loving heart and a cheerful countenance! I reached out to my church, to a local Christian college, and my circle of friends and found young women who had somewhat flexible schedules, so they could be available sixteen to twenty hours a week, just four hours at a time, to give me a little break. While they were there, *they* would be the one to get the drink. *They* changed the adult diaper, helped with feeding, etc., at least some of the time. At one point, Troy, a nephew of mine, came and simply sat with my wife so that I could go to sleep for a few hours! (This young man literally saved my life.)

Something to think about:

First, don't be afraid to ask. Those who love you and those who are *really* your friends will find a way to help you, even if in the smallest of ways. Think of things that would be a huge break for you, and ask for that kind of help. I found that if a neighbor would sit with my wife for an hour so I could go to the grocery store, it was a *huge* mental and emotional break!

Second, what you need is wisdom beyond what you have in your natural mind, for sure! In James 1:5, God's Word says, "Now if any of you lacks wisdom, he should ask God, who gives generously to all without finding fault." Don't think that this is just some nice little fable from the Bible; it's *true.* Get in a quiet place, and ask God for wisdom. Notice that God's Word adds that little phrase, *"without finding fault."*

Let's pray:

Our Lord, we should always be coming to you *first* with our cares and needs. But too many times we say, "Well, we've tried everything else, so all we have left is to pray!" We know that you love us and care about us, and you're not some aloof power that is not in touch with our feelings! No! You are our Abba Father, our provider, our support, our guide, and the leader of our lives! Father, I pray that you will give the reader truly supernatural wisdom in their situation and that you will make yourself very real to them right now! *Amen!*

Chapter 5

What Happens If...?

Family and friends often scold me when I would do things which in most people's lives would be considered normal, like hanging Christmas lights on the exterior of our home or even getting on the ladder in the house to change a high light bulb. They would say, "What would you do if you fell and hurt yourself? Who would take care of Diana? What would happen to your business?" I came to realize, it's not that they don't believe I'm capable of handling those types of tasks because I'm old and decrepit and senile (haha!), but instead it's because the consequences of an injury for *me* are far greater than for most others. My wife's safety and well-being were linked to mine.

Well, one fateful day, I got a taste of those consequences. I fell. Hard. Diana had already been rolled into the van, and her wheelchair locked into place. I zipped back into the house to get her morning medications, which I had somehow forgotten to give her during breakfast. As I came down the ramp in the garage, I stepped on a wet, almost-frozen patch of concrete and slipped. I did a Charlie Brown–style fall, and I landed somehow with my right leg twisted under my backside. The moment I hit the ground, a searing pain shot through my entire body, and I nearly blacked out. I can honestly say, I don't recall ever experiencing that much pain!

I lay there for what seemed like an eternity, trying to catch my breath and trying not to pass out. I remember thinking, *Phil, you have to do something. Diana is sitting alone in that van, and it's very cold. You can't pass out!* After a few moments, I dragged myself to the wheel well of the van and used the tire to help get up to my knees, which was an incredibly painful but necessary action! I decided that I needed to get into the driver's seat where I could rest and also be able to turn on the car to get the heater going for Diana. It took me a long while to get into the driver's seat. And after a while I thought, *Okay, well, you made it this far. Go ahead and take that prescription to the drive-through pharmacy, and get it turned in for Diana.* I realized quickly that I couldn't use my right foot on the pedals, so I drove with my left foot. The dashboard announced that I was almost out of gas, so I decided to go ahead and try to fill the car since I would be right there at the grocery store gas station next to the pharmacy. (I figured I could hop on one leg if necessary.) I pulled into the gas station and found the pump I needed, and with breathless pain, I eased myself out and shut the door to preserve heat in the van for Diana. Once the car was filled, I went to get back into the van and discovered to my horror that the doors were locked. And, yes, right there hanging in the ignition were the keys, also locked in the car! There was Diana, looking at me through the glass, not quite understanding and unable to communicate. I knew I needed help. Whispering a prayer under my breath, I grabbed my phone from my pocket to call my brother, Homer, to come rescue us, only to find that I'd let the battery drain completely! It was dead as a doornail!

I hopped across the gas station parking lot and into the warmth of the lobby and explained to the attendant, who quickly offered his phone. I realized that I have never bothered to memorize anyone's phone numbers…after all, they are in the autodial memory on the phone! The attendant, seeing that I was really concerned and also in a lot of pain, said, "Okay, how about this: Since you have an Android phone like mine, you can sit in my car for a few minutes and charge your phone on my car charger." What an amazing blessing! Once the phone had a minimal charge, I called my brother, who was always anxious to help me, but it went to phone mail. Next, I reached out to my nephew, Troy. He was actually on the way to my house to pick up something he needed and had literally driven past that gas station a few minutes prior! I told him the garage door code to our home and where the spare set of keys to the van were kept. He raced there, got in, grabbed the spare car key set, and raced back to the gas station. Diana was cold and confused but safe.

Something to think about:

Oh, you *think* you have control of things, but every once in a while, life shows you otherwise! When you put your faith in God, you have a friend who is truly closer than a brother. He's promised to go with us through our difficulties but *not* to keep us out of difficulties. When the troubles come, *praise* him for his care, love and concern! Even in our most-challenging times, if we can keep our eyes on *him*, we will find that we are able to get through them.

Let's pray:

Lord, your Word reminds us that you are indeed a friend who is near to us and "sticks closer than a brother" (Proverbs 18:24). You have promised never to leave us or forsake us (Deuteronomy 31:8). I pray that during the reader's darkest times, your Holy Spirit will remind them to lift their eyes up to you because *you* are the true joy giver, and you'll be with us always! Amen!

Chapter 6

Phil's Paraphrase of Romans 8:35–39

Caregivers, even those of us who put up a good front, are seeming plagued by constant new challenges and difficulties that can be crushing. We worry about our lack of skills, our fatigue, our finances, our relationships, but Romans 8:35–39 puts that all into perspective.

This famous portion of Scripture is wonderful, as written. No doubt about that! However, what if we were to paraphrase it in the context of our world today and the challenges we face as caregivers? Here is my paraphrase of some important verses from God's Word:

Romans 8:35–36: Who is it that can actually keep us from Christ's love? What about all this difficulty in our life, like viruses, financial problems, no budget for clothes for the kids, or hunger? What about injuries and our loved one's illness or disability? What about people who threaten us, like it says in Psalm 44:22? What about war? What about election results? What about inflation?

Romans 8:37: Absolutely, *none* of that can keep us from his love! God's Word says that we are winners—*huge* winners—because of the fact that it's *Christ* who has the battle! The battle you are facing truly belongs to the Lord! (Christ says, "Don't worry, I've got this because of how much I love you!")

Romans 8:38: Because I read God's word, and because I listen to his Holy Spirit speaking to me, I can know positively that death or life, even powerful angels or demons, don't have the strength needed to separate us from God's love! And what about worries concerning the present and of the future? *Nope!* Put them directly into Christ's hands because he has promised to fight all the powers that come against us of any kind.

Romans 8:39: So here's the way it is. This is a fact. Nothing up in the heavens or in the depth of the sea or any creature in all of creation has what it takes to separate us from the love of God that is in Christ Jesus our Lord.

Something to think about:

God, in his mercy and love, already knew the hardships that you and I would face in our lives. One might say, "Well, if he is all-powerful, how come he doesn't just keep us out of hardships?" The answer is that God made us to have a free will, free to choose who we will serve in our lives. What he promised is that in life, when we have hardships, he will walk with us. Psalm 23 teaches us that even when we "walk through the valley of the shadow of death," he is with us to comfort us and to guide us, *not* to remove us from hardship. Through hardship, our character is built, our faith is increased, and our wisdom is multiplied.

Let's pray:

Father, teach us to trust you! Draw *near* to the reader right now, and comfort them, guide them…give them your wisdom in their situation. Your Word is filled with promises of your abiding love and comfort. You know us, you created us, and you have a *plan* for us— to *bless* us, not to harm us! We thank you in advance for hearing us and acting on our behalf! Amen!

Chapter 7

The "Helmet of Salvation"

It was the third time we had heard the suggestion from one doctor or another, "Diana, would you consider wearing some sort of head protection?"

There are milestones that we all achieve in our lives; some are good, some are, well, difficult. I remember when my dear father had to give up driving. I remember when my mother was no longer able to walk. It appeared we were at another milestone. We struggle to keep from moving from that which is familiar, that which we know. But inevitably, time marches on, and Diana's Huntington's disease was progressing. The most visible effects were associated with motor skills. Diana would fall constantly. We did everything we could think of to compensate, like putting antislip surface on the bottoms of her shoes and eliminating obvious trip hazards, but her falls were more and more frequent and were getting really dangerous. Combine the reduced motor skills with a loss of reasoning and logic, and you are going to see lots of injuries!

As with every other aspect of Huntington's disease, Diana faced this with grace.

We decided that the helmet she would wear would be a bike helmet because it looked more normal, and she wouldn't have to feel like everyone was looking at her. We went to a bicycle shop, where she picked out a helmet. We bought cute little stickers that she liked to personalize it. When she put it on for the first time, I remember she looked at me, sighed, and said, "I fall down. I get up." She buckled the little strap below her chin, and we drove home.

It turned out to be a *very* good decision to use that helmet. I can't even count the number of times that Diana fell, struck her head, and had nothing injured but her pride.

Something to think about:

Changes *will* come in our lives. Being a caregiver has taught me that it's *never* about the change that is happening; it's about how you handle the change that counts. What matters is that we must recognize that there is no situation that happens to us that comes as a surprise to God. *Never* does God say, "Wow, I didn't see that coming!" For those who trust God, the events of their lives are truly "God filtered." Know that God is good all the time and that he has a plan for our lives. How we respond will either build our faith or destroy it. Diana had learned this lesson well.

Let's pray!

God, please give us the wisdom and the grace to accept the changes in our lives, knowing that you walk with us! You have commanded your angels to guard us in all our ways (Psalm 91:11). Bless us "coming in and going out," and let our lives be a testimony to your power and your provision. *Amen!*

Chapter 8

I Was "Short" with Her Again!

I can't believe it! How could I be so selfish, so lame! She's the one that has Huntington's, not me, so why can't I be more patient! I know I should be more patient, but how can I make that happen? I'm not wired that way! These and a thousand other self-condemning thoughts raced through my mind often and especially at the moment where, through fatigue and loneliness, I responded badly to the situation that presented itself.

No amount of teaching or reading of the educational literature really prepared me for when it became personal. Oh, sure, when I read it, I understood it completely. "When the individual with Huntington's disease demonstrates irrational behavior, it is fruitless to attempt to 'reason' with them about it because *to them*, what they are doing is perfectly rational and reasonable." But then…my wife comes walking out of the bathroom with her pants around her ankles (not understanding that she forgot to pull them up)…a huge trip hazard just *begging* for a fall and possible injury! (Gee, I wonder why I can't rely upon all that wonderful teaching about "how to act"?) Instead, I blurted out, "Diana! Don't do that! Don't you know how dangerous that is?" Uh, no, she does *not* know how dangerous it is, and my outburst served no useful purpose whatsoever but to frustrate her and cause her stress. *Then*…the condemnation piles on yet again, *Why did I yell at her?* Multiply this over and over again all day, all week, all month, and all year, and the self-condemnation piles up.

My brother, Homer, is such a blessing, and I love being able to open up to him when I'm needing a safe place to talk. One time, when he was visiting our house, he and I were sitting in the family room, watching TV, and Diana came into the room. Sure enough, she somehow tripped and began to fall. I leapt out of my recliner, but the distance was too great, and her fall was already in progress. Out of my mouth came a loud "Nooooo! Darn it, Diana!" And after a few minutes, my brother said, "Phil, you really need to figure out how to respond so that you don't panic all the time! It's stressful to both Diana and to you!" He is *so* right, of course, but…I tried to explain it to him like this: "How about if I tell you that I'm going to burn you with a match, and I won't warn you before I do it, do you suppose you would not ever flinch and shout out? And what if I burned you with a match every five minutes for the next several days? Would you eventually get used to it so that you reacted calmly every time the flame touched your skin?" That's how it felt to me. No matter how much I rationalize that she *will* fall down and much of the time it cannot be helped, that didn't lessen my panic when I saw the love of my life on her way to the floor.

Something to think about:

Life as a caregiver of a loved one is guaranteed to be filled with unending opportunities for God to grow you in the area of patience and faith. I made it a constant matter of prayer that God would use these difficult life lessons to grow my wisdom, understanding, and patience, while there was still time to demonstrate grace in my life, in the way I treated my sweet wife, as well as others!

Let's pray!

God, thank you that *you* know how to care for what belongs to you, and my wife and I belong to you! Please flood my life with your amazing *grace* so that I can turn my panic into solid, caring action. Help me change my fear of not being able to protect my wife into a *trust* in the fact that you are ultimately the one who is Diana's protector! Take away my self-condemnation, Lord. I know that in your Word in Romans 8:1, You tell us this: "Therefore, there is now no condemnation for those who are in Christ Jesus…" So help me to take that teaching to heart, Lord! *Amen*!

Chapter 9

Swimming in Her Robe and Helmet

Years ago, I had a recurring nightmare. I don't remember much of the dream, except for one vivid, terrible image. In my dream, I was standing beside a body of water. And looking down, I could see my wife, Diana, below the surface, and her eyes were locked on mine, frightened and wide as she sank deeper and deeper, away from my grasp. I'm pretty sure the dream was an analogy for her Huntington's disease and the feeling of helplessness I had, knowing that I could not save her, try as I might.

Unexpectedly, one day, that dream almost became a reality.

We arrived home from church one Sunday, and Diana disappeared into the restroom while I changed clothes. I was looking forward to planting the tomatoes and peppers that I had purchased a couple of weeks earlier. Diana reappeared from the restroom in her swimsuit and asked if I would go to the hot tub by the pool with her. I'll admit, I was frustrated because I wanted to spend just that little bit of time for myself, gardening.

After thinking about it for a moment, I made a compromise. "Diana, how about if I help you into the hot tub, and I'll be right there, only twenty feet away. I'll be watching carefully in case you need some help, okay?" (You see, at this point in time, Diana was

21

unable to sit up very well by herself, so in the hot tub, we would put a "noodle" around her, under her arms, to help her stay upright.) She was happy to get her hot tub time, so off we went. I assisted her into the hot tub, held her firmly until she was seated in the place she was safest, and then went over and began my joyful (although somewhat distracted) gardening. After getting only two tomato plants in the ground, I saw that she was motioning for me. She was done already! Barely five minutes! I trotted over there and did our usual drill associated with extracting her from the hot tub: right hand on the hot tub handhold, left foot over the side and onto the relative safety of the step. My left hand was on her right hand so her hand would remain firmly on the handhold, and my right hand was on her waist to steady her as she stepped out completely. Then we backed her down the two steps to the stone pool decking. As soon as she was steady, I draped a towel over her shoulders and helped dry her back. Then she wrapped the towel around her waist, and I slipped a big terry cloth robe onto her shoulders. Next, without fail, we always had the same discussion, "Diana, please, *please* wait for me. Don't walk away without me. Let me slip the cover back on the hot tub, and we'll walk back to the house."

The path from the hot tub to the house includes a very narrow point between the pool and a large planter of roses. *Naturally*, Diana took off without me and was about three strides ahead of me when my nightmare began to unfold just like in my dream!

As she walked around the pool, she wobbled then careened sideways into the pool. I thought, *Man is she going to be cold! That water is still only around fifty degrees!* In the split seconds it took for me to think that, to my horror, I saw her sinking into the deepest part of the pool. From about two feet below the surface, her wide, frightened eyes locked on mine as she struggled with her arms and legs, to no avail, the bulky robe and towel wrapping and tangling her limbs. I kicked off my shoes and jumped in as close as possible to her position and shot past her to the bottom, thinking that I would push off the bottom to come up under her, and that would help push her to the surface.

When I came up to her from below, I slipped my left arm around her at about the knees and began to kick and swim with my free arm toward the surface. That's when I realized that my bulking clothing, plus Diana's robe, towel, and protective helmet were making progress in the water almost impossible. For the first time, the thought raced through my mind that I might fail, that I might lose her!

I tore at that towel around her waist and pulled it off, then got the robe off her shoulders and again pushed toward the surface. I popped *her* head above the water and thought, *Okay, now I can let go and get to the surface myself, and I'll grab her again.* The moment I let go, she began to sink quickly, so I grabbed her once more from below and just kept kicking toward the edge of the pool. In what seemed like an eternity, I got to the edge and popped up beside her. My left arm was around her waist now. I got a firm grasp on the stone decking at the edge of the pool and pulled us both to safety at the side. We were coughing and sputtering as I used my right hand to pull us along to the shallower end of the pool until I caught my footing on the bottom.

I said, "Diana, will you wait for me now?" I hugged her, and we lumbered up the pool steps out of that water. I got her over to a deck chair and sat her down so that she could dry off a little. When she emerged from the water, we both laughed when we saw that during the entire event, she never let go of the Starbucks cup in her left hand! It was full of pool water but still in her feisty grip! We sat there and prayed, thanking the Lord for the ultimate, safe outcome of this very scary event!

Something to think about:

When you find yourself sinking" into despair, look up toward God and see that he is reaching for you! Don't allow discouragement and fatigue to pull you under! Instead, draw close to God, spend time in prayer, and allow God to flow peace into your life. I'm reminded of the wonderful old hymn by James Rowe and Howard E. Smith, penned in 1912 and based on Matthew chapter 14, "I was sinking deep in sin, far from the peaceful shore, very deeply stained within, sinking to rise no more! Then the master of the sea heard my despairing cry, from the waters lifted me, now safe am I! Love lifted me; love lifted me! When nothing else could help, love lifted me!"

Let's pray!

Father God, thank you for your amazing care and guidance during frightening situations! Lord, thank you for protecting my wife so many times and for giving me a calm spirit so I could deal with the many challenging situations in our lives! Never let me forget that *you* sent your Son, Jesus, to rescue *me* from the deep waters of an eternity without you! Amen!

Chapter 10

Faster than a Speeding Bullet

I was always quick to try any implement, aid, or tool that might make everyday life easier for my wife and me, as we lived each day in an ever evolving "new normal." So when I had the opportunity to purchase an electric mobility chair, I jumped at it! I said to myself, "After all, what if this was the thing that reduced her frequent falls?"

After months of practice and becoming accustomed to the chair, Diana was accepting of it, although not happy about its presence in her life. I found that with time, she became more familiar and comfortable with the controls, however the advancing Huntington's disease seemed to have offset any improvements in her control of the chair in recent months.

I had recently painted all the interior doors in our house because after years of wear, they were really in need of an overhaul. A nice fresh coat of high-gloss, white paint really freshened things up! Diana liked to "roll" down into my office at the end of the hall with her electric mobility chair just to see what I was up to or to have me address a card she would like to send. Even though the door to my office was a "straight shot" down the hallway for her, no turns needed, the door and woodwork entering my office seem to be taking an unusual beating because of the frequency of her visits. (I *truly loved* having her in my office…usually…but that's another story!)

Each time I walked in and out that door, I smiled and thought about the fact that just a few short weeks ago, the door was pristine and beautiful—perfect paint, no dings or scrapes. "I need to just put it on the calendar as a task to do monthly," I told myself. I'd just do touch-up painting around the house on some certain Saturday of each month. Still it's another one of those tasks that had intensified over the prior six months.

On this day, she came into my office while I was on a conference call. I motioned *shhhhh* with my index finger to my lips, and she pulled up beside my desk in the very most narrow area. I thought to myself, *Oh, of course she came into this spot that is impossible to back out of carefully, and here I am on the phone.* She sat and listened for a bit, then began to look around like, *This is boring. How am I going to get out of here?* So I quietly stood and used the little joystick on the arm of the mobility chair to guide her backward. I noted it was *really* moving slowly due to the area rug in my office, so I nudged the speed dial up to about three-quarters, and that chair backed right out of there rather briskly! (Note to self: I needed to remember in the future that reverse speeds on those chairs are *much* slower than forward at the same setting!)

I aimed her chair toward the door to my office as kind of a hint that I really needed to have some peace so that I could finish the conference call.

Suddenly, the chair *lurched* forward and crashed violently into the office door, crushing it and breaking it in half at about two feet from the bottom! Diana had the cutest deer-in-the-headlights' look on her sweet face, and I couldn't help but laugh out loud right there on the conference call! I'm sure the others on the call thought I was crazy, but it was worth it!

Something to think about:

When we are living in the moment, sometimes it's difficult to recognize that a memory is being made. Ask God to give you the wisdom and grace to recognize *more* of these moments, and savor them.

There will come a time in your life where those memories will be a cherished blessing for you!

Let's pray!

Lord, *thank you* for giving me the gift of *time* with my wife! I pray that you will always help me to see past the temporal and meaningless things, like that insignificant door, and to keep my heart focused on the eternal things, like the spirit and soul of my Diana. Let me be a blessing to my wife during this difficult and challenging season of her life. I want to honor *you*, Father, by the way I respond to the unexpected incidents that come along. Help me always to respond in patience and love, and help me develop character in my life! *Amen!*

Chapter 11

Too Protective—Not Protective Enough...

Our church in Berkeley, California, was hosting a wonderful event we call "Church in the Park." Our little church was a growing and enthusiastic congregation of around fifty, and we were anxious to make a difference in our community by reaching out to people living there. This event (the week prior to Easter) was held at a city park only a few blocks from our church. We had inflatable jumpers for the kids, Easter eggs, free sandwiches and drinks, and live music provided by our church worship team. All of our married lives, Diana and I had been right in the heart of this type of exciting ministry, doing anything that needed done. So a few weeks prior, it was almost instinctive for Diana to want to sign up as one of the helpers.

I must admit that when I saw her over there in her wheelchair at the sign-up table, I groaned inside. (*Now that I think of it, I hope that the groan was "inside" and wasn't heard by all around me!*) One of the things that is so tough about Huntington's disease is that the person with the disease simply *doesn't realize* how much the disease is affecting their ability to do things. Add to that the challenges to judgment that are common with the disease, and you find people with Huntington's many times attempting things that are simply outside of their ability to handle, either physically, cognitively, or both. The only thing I could think of was, *Great. Now what? I can't simply not go because we want to support this ministry and help make it successful.*

I knew that it was likely that when Diana and I went to help at the event, I would spend most of my time there trying to keep Diana from wandering off, falling, or otherwise attempting to do something that would put her at risk.

A funny thing happened that morning however. While getting dressed early Sunday morning and doing Diana's hair, I got a "whisper" from God. Not an audible voice, mind you, but the impression in my heart was *very* solid, "Phil, don't worry. Diana will be safe. She needs to help with this ministry. *You* need to help with this ministry. Go, and it will be okay."

Our friend Sheila came along, and that was a wonderful blessing because she and Diana were able to spend time together, and I had a little less to worry about regarding Diana's safety.

When the inflatable jumpers were blown up, and the band started playing, the people started coming. Moms and dads with toddlers, college students from the university, and homeless folks began filling the park! (There are plenty of homeless folks in Berkeley!) Our pastor got the helpers all together at the food tent and handed us all flyers about our church, along with a CD of music from our worship team and told us, "Okay, this is why we did this event...to reach out to our community! Let's all get out there and meet them and hand out flyers and CDs and tell them we appreciate their coming to our event!" Diana had such difficulty walking and was typically "unsafe at any speed" when out of her wheelchair, but she got up out of that chair, like a bullet, and grabbed a handful of those flyers, and off she went, wobbling and weaving, wearing her helmet, into the crowd with a huge smile on her glowing face.

I froze. My instant reaction was to go to her side and take her arm and maybe escort her to the safety of her wheelchair. But I remembered God's whisper of the morning and allowed his peace to replace the anxiety. Instead, I watched as she approached person after person. And although many of them might or might not have fully understood what she said with her *words*, it was unmistakable what she was saying with her heart. Her face conveyed it all, "I am *so happy* to see you here! *Thank you* for coming! I would like to give you this gift of a music CD from our church!" I didn't see one person turn her away. How *could* they, with that glowing face?

Something to think about:

When you're faced with a challenging event or a tough decision, how do you react? What's your first thought? I strive daily to turn my thought life over to God to actually *allow* him to be the leader of my life. But how can he be the leader of my life if I don't *listen* to that still, small voice and then *submit* to his leading in my life? I'd urge you today to trust the God of the universe, who loves you and cares about you. He is faithful to care for you in every area of your life and relationships.

Let's pray!

Father God, forgive me for not trusting you with my darling wife, with my emotions, and with my life. You have promised never to leave me or forsake me. You've promised to go with me through the storms of life. You've promised that your *grace* is sufficient! Lord, *thank you* for teaching me this lesson through the joy and service of my wife, who overcame what most would consider a huge disability and went fearlessly into that crowd to share your love! Amen!

Chapter 12

The Annual Huntington's Show-and-Tell Session

Each year in August, we visited the Huntington's Center of Excellence in San Francisco at UCSF or in Omaha at the University of Nebraska, where they have assembled a highly trained group of specialists who are focused on treatment and eventually the cure of Huntington's disease. For the first few years after Diana and I agreed to do the genetic testing for a solid diagnosis, the visits were lengthy and very involved. Many times, a team of medical students came along as a learning experience. Diana *absolutely loved* the entire process and would do her best to explain to the students what she was feeling, sensing, and thinking about. They were always taken aback by her wonderful, cheerful, godly attitude!

There are a series of predictive tests that are almost always administered in order to measure the progression of Huntington's disease. Some are tactical, requiring the use of fingers, hands, walking, and other motor skills. Then there are the mental acuity tests… (And I am so glad that I *don't* have to pass them!) They showed her a series of eight or ten words and then asked her to repeat them back to them fifteen minutes later. They showed her the word *green* written with red ink and asked her to say what color it was, and on and on and on.

Some years, Diana would do quite well, and the doctors would say to her, "Diana, you are having a good year! We're really happy for you!" And then they always followed up with, "Now it's important for you to understand that just because your symptoms seem to be holding and not increasing, that does not mean that you are getting better." Nice. Well, I understand that they can't be giving patients a false sense that, somehow, they are "beating" what they believe is an "unbeatable" death sentence, but it is hard for a husband to hear nonetheless. This never fazed Diana. At least if it did, she certainly never showed it. A big smile and sometimes even a hug for a nurse—Diana was a joy giver. Years ago, at the end of one of these examinations, Diana gave the doctor and all the attendants gospel tracts because she wanted to share with them where her *joy* came from. (I was one proud husband!)

After the lengthy examination, we always made it a point to spend some time in downtown San Francisco, seeing the sights, eating someplace fun, and just being together. For me it was a time of decompression. For Diana, it was part of what allowed her to look forward with joyful anticipation to this annual ritual at the University of California–San Francisco.

Something to think about:

I learned so *much* from my wife's amazing character, how she treated others and from the grace she exhibited in the midst of a life experience that most people could not even imagine. I was humbled to see all the instances where she would stop to pray for someone, give things to people in need, and generally just pour out her spirit onto the world.

We need to learn to *add value*. In every interaction and every situation, try to *add value*. Learn to serve others, and *you* will be uplifted and blessed in spite of your life's challenges. The more you give, the bigger your heart becomes. Take a lesson from 1 Thessalonians 5:11, where it says, "So encourage each other and build each other up…"

Let's pray!

Father, *how* did this woman retain such a joyful outlook? Lord, I know it was from you because she told me so often! Dear God, I saw through her life the demonstration of how you give "joy in the morning" to those who hunger for your love and who seek your face!

Dear reader, his favor lasts a lifetime. "Weeping may remain for a night, but rejoicing comes in the morning" (Psalm 30:5b). *Amen*!

Chapter 13

Emergency Room…Again

I was suddenly awakened at about 4:00 a.m. on a Sunday morning to a thud sound… My mind quickly tried to acclimate, reaching for the lamp switch. Diana was not in bed with me! I leapt out of bed, and racing around to her side of the bed, I found Diana on the floor, next to the bed, in fetal position. I knelt quickly, asking her the usual questions, "Are you hurt?" "Did you hit your head when you fell?" And suddenly, I realized that my hand was wet, and it was blood from her scalp. I rushed to the bathroom, grabbed a wash-cloth, and rushed back to apply pressure, breathing a prayer, "Father God, please protect my Diana!" After inspection, with good light, I could see it was only about an inch long but bleeding profusely, more of a cut than I could properly care for at home. So we headed out to the emergency room, less than a mile from our home.

We entered the lobby of the emergency room, and the endless forms and questions began. Diana was quickly separated from me and was asked if she had any reason that she might be "unsafe at home" (not-so-thinly-veiled code for *"Did your husband do this to you?"*). The sights, sounds, and smells of the emergency room were too familiar to me. Diana seemed to relish the attention and was a superb patient, very cooperative! I presented the attending nurse with my laminated list of medications she was taking, which they appreciated and entered into the records while another nurse applied triage to the wound. The doctor arrived and recognized us and used the specialized equipment to close the wound with four bright and shiny stainless-steel staples. Diana was thankful that they didn't need to shave part of her head this time. The doctor gave me a surgical staple remover and said, "You've been through this so often. If you like, you can remove the staples when the wound is healed. It will save you a trip to the doctor."

Four stainless-steel staples later and we are on our way home. I was drained emotionally, but it was so important for me to smile, encourage Diana... Diana was *such* a trooper and never ceased to amaze me! Then Diana surprised me yet again; she said, "Looks like we will go ahead and make it to church this morning!"

And all that morning, I had thought that it was up to *me* to be the encourager!

Something to think about:

We think that we, as the caregivers, are the ones who lend support and strength, but if we allow God to soften our hearts to be receptive, we'll find that often it is our loved one that is providing us with that support and strength! Never forget that God has a plan for the life of your loved one too, and God might just be giving *them* a ministry of encouragement that they can only share through a smile or hug of your hand. Ask God to show you what your loved one's ministry is, if they are unable to tell you. When God reveals that to you, encourage your loved one in that, as it will change your life!

Let's pray!

Dear Lord, what a blessing you had given me to have this amazing and strong woman at my side! Teach me through her, Lord. Let her serve you by the example of trust and faith that she demonstrated to me and to the world around her. Mortal man has such a total misunderstanding of what *true strength is*, but this precious, fragile woman shows us all how a godly woman responds to adversity. Give her joy in her day, Father, and stimulate her ability to minister to others in ways that only she can!

Chapter 14

Did I Really Have That Thought Just Now? Why Am I So Angry?

There were two entire years where my wife, Diana, was passing through a terrible stage of Huntington's disease, when it is common for HD patients to become so frustrated and angry with their utterly helpless situation that they act out in terrible ways. Since she could no longer form more than two- or three-word sentences or put together any kind of cry for help that could be understood, she would instead just scream. And scream. And scream. Sometimes she would scream at the top of her lungs for six hours at a time until she literally became so exhausted that she could no longer carry on. If I came near her during those rants, she would try to hit, bite, or do anything to express her anger and frustration. As her husband and caregiver, this really crushed me physically, emotionally, and spiritually. Honestly, I didn't want to live. I truly thought that there was no hope, no way out, and that nothing was ever going to get better. During those times, my thoughts were dark. Thoughts crossed my mind, like, *I just want to hurt her. I hate her. I wish she would just die!* I share this with you because if you are a caregiver in an intense situation, you *will* have these thoughts, and you need to make a plan for how to escape those dark thoughts that *will* come. You need to recognize that you are not alone. It's during our weakest, most-fatigued moments that the enemy of our soul speaks to our minds. When that happens, call out to God (and to friends or family at that moment).

On a lighter note, during one of these long screaming sessions, after Diana had been screaming for many hours, I finally got right in her face. And when she took a breath so she could scream more, I said in a frustrated tone, "Diana! You're just screaming and screaming!" Suddenly, she looked surprised. And instead of screaming, she shouted, "No kidding, Jack!" It took me by such surprise that I began to laugh, and she laughed as well. And then...she went back to screaming.

Something to think about:

When you find yourself at the end of your rope, *change things*. That may sound too simple, but it is effective. Don't just "hang in there." Get help so that you don't snap. During times of extreme stress and fatigue, you sink to thoughts that are *unhealthy* for both you and your loved one. Make a deal with your pastor, your family member, anyone you can really trust, that if you call and say the end-of-my-rope signal, they will come to you at once. Don't think you are somehow tough enough to just make it through. It's nothing to treat lightly. If you start to think that the only way out is your death or the death of your loved one, you need help at once, not tomorrow morning.

Let's pray:

Dear Lord, during the dark times, reveal yourself in a mighty way to the reader. Give them a sense of peace and love that only you are able to provide. Let your Holy Spirit bring people alongside them so they know they are cared for. Amen!

Chapter 15

Combating Loneliness and Isolation

As time goes on, the needs of our loved one grows. If it's an aging parent, a spouse with cancer, or any other situation that requires increasing attention and time, we find that no matter how hard we try, we don't seem to be able to get any more than twenty-four hours out of a day or seven days out of a week. My job was growing more and more demanding at the same time as my wife's care requirements were increasing, and I was truly at the end of my rope, trying to do it all. With a lot of prayer and planning, I just pulled the plug on my career. And after twenty-five years with my company, I resigned. I honestly didn't know what I would do because at age fifty, there I was, unemployed and without any source of income. I knew God would not abandon me, but God *also* expects us to do our part and work hard. He will help us find favor with others and will help smooth the way, but we still are in charge of the doing. I had the savings that I'd always thought would be our retirement, but now I was just thanking God that I'd saved all my life so that now I had at least a little time to build some sort of income. Over a couple of years, I finally had developed an online supply business that was able to provide our basic needs and allow me to work from home so I could care for Diana full-time.

But that's not what this chapter is about. During this period, where I'd moved on from my career and focused upon caring for Diana while at the same time trying to build the work-from-home business, I came to recognize, I was becoming *isolated*. I wasn't trying to, but my only real contacts with other adults were doctors, nurses, pharmacists, and occasional delivery people. I hungered for conversation that was not care related. I wanted to be able to do more in my home-based business so that I would have that contact, but frankly, it just wasn't there. I found myself skipping church and justifying it because of my care responsibilities, but frankly, that was a lame excuse. I could have gone. But the more time I spent at home with just my wife and me, the more anxious I was becoming about being out in public.

I can assure you that allowing yourself to withdraw from the rest of the world is a recipe for disaster. We are social creatures. God made us to have companionship. And even from the very beginning, he said, "It is not good for man to be alone" (Genesis 2:18). I didn't realize how much trouble I was in emotionally and physically until one day at one of Diana's update doctor's visit at the University of Nebraska. They brought in a clinical psychologist who *really* straightened me out. He told me that he wanted me to arrange to have at least two times a week where I would spend an hour with my brother at a coffee shop and another two hours where someone would sit with Diana and allow me to walk around in a Walmart or some other mindless activity. I followed his instructions, and it was life-changing. In that way, I became able to face my day, my week, my life!

Something to think about:

When you find yourself in an almost superhuman set of responsibilities, don't isolate yourself. Don't withdraw from your family, your church, your friends. You don't have to change everything at once, but *do* make positive changes that are designed to take care of yourself. You are of *no good* at all to your loved one if you begin to implode!

Let's pray:

Lord, help us to learn to lean upon you, to trust your many promises! You'll be a friend who is closer than a brother. You are a strong tower into which we can run for safety. You are our provider, our comforter, our Savior! Help us to have the courage to reach out when we are hurting. Please cause someone near to us to come up beside us in this difficult walk, just to be here for us. Most of all, Father, please make yourself incredibly *real* to us right now! Amen.

Chapter 16

Feelings of Inadequacy for the Task God Has for Me

I'm so frustrated. I'm doing the best I can, but I can't keep up. I know God has me in this situation so that I can be his arms extended and his love expressed. I love the thought of that role, but I feel I am so inadequate! I want to believe that I'm doing what God wants me to do, but there is so much on my shoulders that I fear I'll make mistakes that I could have avoided! I need God's direction and wisdom in my life so that I can do my best for my beloved wife! She counts on me and trusts me so... I just need to make it another day, another week! I feel like asking God if, somehow, I misunderstood his plan for my life! Am I doing it right? Am I doing all I can? What if I fail?!

Sometimes the reality and the weight of your responsibilities seem just overwhelming. Late at night, after things have slowed down, the thoughts begin to flow in. *Diana would be helpless without me. What would happen to her? If I'm not beside her every moment, she might fall, and it would be my fault for not being there at the right moment. If she were in a nursing home, would anyone care about her, visit her? If she chokes because I'm not watching, that would be my fault!*

Who would do the special things only I know she likes? Who would protect her? Who would handle all the paperwork with her doctors?

The truth of it is, the answers to those type of questions are all over the place. Some of her special things would just go away. To avoid falls, she might be restrained. The prospect of my beloved wife without me to fight for her was just too much to contemplate. To make matters worse, sometimes family and friends would say things like, "Phil, your wife just wouldn't make it very long without you!" Naturally, they intended this as a compliment, but it just reinforced my fears!

Something to think about:

Remember what God's Word says about these feelings of inadequacy; he says, "Be brave because I am with you" (Joshua 1:9). We can do *all* things through Christ, who strengthens us. You've said that you are our High Priest who *does* understand our feelings and infirmities… but that you are truly touched personally. Trust him in all your ways, and he will go before you.

Let's Pray:

God, you know me better than any human could ever know me. You said that you knew me before the beginning of time and had already planned good works for me to accomplish in your name! (Read Ephesians 2:10!) Father, I pray that you will wash over my fears, like a mighty flood of love and comfort, cause me to turn from fear to trust, from hurt to joy. Spring up a well within my soul, and help me to *praise* you in every situation! Amen.

Chapter 17

She Laughed Today

I remember one time when I realized that the day had been without any Huntington problems at all—truly a rarity. I said to myself, "Today, my Diana did so well. She didn't fall, she didn't choke, and we were able to communicate pretty well." I realized that afternoon how I need to accept this type of victory for what it is, a gift from God of a good day.

One of the things that I had learned about Diana's disease, she wasn't able to smile or laugh on command. When you saw her smile or if she laughed, it was *real* and from her heart. You might be surprised to know how many times you smile because you feel it's the right thing to do: to smile at someone who smiles at you or chuckle when someone tells a dumb joke. So it made people uncomfortable sometimes when they saw Diana, and she did not express any facial expression at all.

It seemed like months since I'd heard her laugh. She had always been full of joy and mischief and laughed easily. However, the phase of her Huntington's disease she was struggling through caused her so much exhaustion and frustration that she seemed to find little occasion to laugh or even smile. Today, I broke through that curtain of difficulty by accident while visiting Olive Garden for dinner. I lifted a large glass of ice tea to my mouth, and suddenly the ice in the glass shifted and slammed forward, spilling what seemed like gallons of tea down the front of my shirt and all over my meal! Sitting there in her wheelchair at the table, she laughed and laughed. And even though dripping wet, I rejoiced inside and laughed with her—a memory to treasure and ponder in my heart even now, decades later in life.

Something to think about:

It might be hard, but try and be the cheerleader for your loved one in their time of difficulty. Don't be a party pooper or a wet blanket when they have even a small joy or victory! And *whatever* you do, don't try to be the voice of reason or try to get them to see the reality of their situation. Believe me, they already know that. What they *need* is someone who will celebrate even the smallest victory and point out the good things that remain.

Let's pray:

Lord God, you are the true joy giver, and you can instill joy in us, even when circumstances appear to be bleak or frustrating. Help us to understand that true *joy* is not dependent upon our happiness but is the state of our spirit. Teach us that having joy is not associated with the right set of circumstances but is a reflection of our trust in you as the giver of life and joy. Help us to focus on the eternal, not the temporary things in our lives. Amen!

Chapter 18

The Mantle of Prayer

Through the years, a very special blessing began to develop in my life. At first, I was only vaguely aware that it was happening and had no concept of how important this blessing would come to be. It was such a comfort to know that in my daily walk, there were those lifting me up to God in prayer for strength to fulfill my caregiver role! Many times, when someone says, "I will remember to pray for you," it's a well-intentioned but sometimes empty promise, not so with a prayer warrior!

My mother had always been a prayer warrior, and I was always humbled when I knew that she truly did pray for me every single day. I didn't know until she was in her eighties that sometimes those prayers were hours long as the Holy Spirit guided her to intercede for my needs. Then, as my wife, Diana, grew older and wiser and more in love with our Heavenly Father, she too became a member of that special club, the prayer warriors, and prayed for me daily with great intensity.

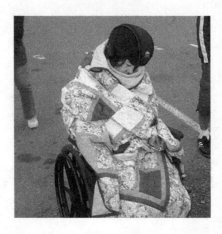

There were many occasions when people would see Diana and think that perhaps she was resting, when in fact she was deep in prayer. I remember one time when our church went to a park to pray for the city of Oakland, and it was rather cold, so Diana was bundled up in a quilt her sister had made for her. She was sitting in her wheelchair, praying. Those who didn't know Diana thought she was sleeping, but *we* knew better!

Without meaning to, I took for granted that I was covered by an invisible mantle of prayer from both my mother and my wife! Many times, I would hear my mother in the wee hours of the morning praying, yearning in earnest, seeking God on my behalf and the behalf of many others. She lived to be 101 and actually died in our home, to be ushered into God's kingdom to sit at the feet of Jesus. Then only a few short years later, my wife died suddenly one morning. No longer would she be lifting me up in prayer! I had lost *both* of those precious women who were covering me with intentional, meaningful prayer! Like a tide washing over me, I was overwhelmed with the realization that no longer did I have *anyone* interceding for me with the Father, asking for favor, asking for my protection, asking for divine guidance for me!

Something to think about:

I fell to my knees and prayed, and God spoke to me. Not an audible voice, mind you, but a very *clear* message came: I was *not* blessed by those women's prayers "just so that I could be blessed and benefited." I was blessed by those lifetimes of prayer so that I could then *become* the prayer mantle for others! There are several who immediately came to mind, and I committed that I would become their prayer warrior and cover them with their own personal mantle of prayer.

As a caregiver, it's so important to get outside of your own problems and cares and intercede for the needs of others. God will bless you and lift up your heart and give you strength for *your* daily battle!

Let's pray!

Father, forgive me for not recognizing what a precious gift I was receiving all those years from two women in my life who loved me dearly! Help me to now carry forward the heritage that has been demonstrated to me so powerfully and so faithfully. Give me patience and wisdom to pray in your spirit so that I will indeed be praying your will for their lives!

Lord, please help the reader to bless others with intercessory prayer and to be faithful to continue, even when it may feel that the prayers are seemingly unanswered. We know that the answer is on the way! Amen.

Chapter 19

Those Feelings of Guilt

Guilt is a challenge that is not often dealt with until long after it begins. You might not even identify your feelings as guilt, but those feelings of self-recrimination sometimes manifest themselves in other forms, such as selfishness or lack of empathy. In the case of a loved one who has a hereditary disease, you might think to yourself, *Why did my sister get the disease and not me? Why was I spared?* If you're caring for your aging father with Alzheimer's, you might be feeling that you're not investing enough time with him. Those small voices in your mind say, "Some son you are. You were disrespectful to your dad all those years, and now look at him! You're a lousy son!" Even if you've hung in there and done a great job caring for your loved one, but now their needs have become greater than what you are capable of providing. Somehow, guilt starts to plague your mind, *Oh, come on. You can do it, but you don't want to! Your love must be pretty weak!* Finally, if you survive your loved one, there's survivor's guilt where you wonder why *you* were allowed to live a full life but not your loved one. It seems that the memories of the occasions, when you failed, are always coming to your remembrance. The *good news* is that all that guilt you've carried on your shoulders for years is false! You need to learn the source of that guilt and drop that baggage on the floor! Believe me, those kinds of destructive thoughts and feelings come from the enemy of our souls, the one who is called the great deceiver. Satan is called the father of lies for a good reason. (Read John 8:44)

Something to think about:

No matter how you came to your situation or how long you've carried that distressing burden of guilt, God is ready with the solution. His arms are outstretched to you. He has promised that he will be with you no matter what, that his Holy Spirit is here to comfort you and guide you! Every *good* gift comes from above, from the Father of light! (Read James 1:17.) The bad things, like guilt and fear, come from the enemy of our soul, the one who is seeking to steal, kill, and destroy. Honestly, it's totally up to you to *choose* life! *Choose joy!*

Let's pray:

Dear Lord, please forgive our impatience, our displays of temper. Please help us to become more and more like Christ! Father, please give us rest in our spirits at the times when we find we are unable to get the rest we need physically. Cause us to have a deep sense of peace in our hearts when it comes to our loved ones, that they are truly in the palm of your hand. And no matter what happens in life, you are with us. You never leave us! Give us wisdom to know how to respond to the unexpected and how to manage our fears. We want to turn our burdens over to you, Father, but it's so hard to let go of them! Thank you for your promises, Lord! Amen!

Chapter 20

Your Roles "Before" and "After"

If the loved one you're caring for is your spouse or significant other, don't let the caregiver role become more important than your role as a life's mate. Sometimes, as caregivers, we tend to reflect upon how it was before our loved one needed so much care—the laughter and spontaneity and the relative ease of daily life. Now, the day-to-day routine can slowly overtake the carefree life that existed before they needed so much care. Before you know it, your thoughts are about preparing medications, scheduling doctor's visits, your loved one's hygiene, and other care requirements. Over time, you might find that romance and intimacy have begun to fade. It's so important to take a step back and realize that you promised to cherish and love them and that they have the same hopes and dreams as they did before.

If your loved one is dealing with a disability where they will gradually lose abilities to communicate or even lose some memories, believe me, they *know* they are declining. It is the source of so much insecurity and fear for them. There are some things that will help both of you retain some of that sense of romance and to demonstrate in a very tangible way that you know who they really are inside. Think about the things that are special to them. For example, my wife loved balloons, swans, lighthouses, and little mouse figurines. She enjoyed

Butterfinger candy bars, gingersnap cookies with orange juice, coconut macaroons, and caramel latte. As she declined, I made sure she sometimes had surprise balloon bouquets and things around her, like the swans and lighthouses that gave her pleasure. They reminded her of *who she was inside*, despite her declining body and mind. When she no longer was able to take food orally, it was so hard! No longer could she eat her favorite things due to choking concerns. I figured out that I could buy food flavorings, like caramel and coconut, and would put just a drop or two of the flavor on a spoon and touch it to her tongue. Her eyes would light up. End even after she was no longer able to respond with a smile, I knew that she was enjoying the sensation and the memories it stimulated.

Something to think about:

One of the most significant things one can do as a caregiver is to help your loved one retain a sense of who they really *are* inside. Encourage them in every way possible. Even when you are tired and discouraged, you can do little things that show them you know them inside. They are so *hungry* to be assured that you know the real them, that you are not allowing their declining physical body to define their identity. And by the way, your acts of kindness and mercy are never overlooked by God.

Let's pray:

Father, forgive me for allowing the challenges of caregiving to erode my relationship with my loved one. Restore to me a sense of love and joy, and flood my spirit with an overwhelming desire to bless and encourage them! Give me a servant's heart! Lord, I know, in your Word, you've said you are near to the brokenhearted (Psalm 34:18) and that you will restore our strength! I'm asking, Father, that you guide me, encourage me, and give me strength for the day! *Amen*!

Chapter 21

It's a Snake Market out There!

We were in our early thirties, and my wife's Huntington's disease was just starting to show symptoms. Huntington's disease (HD) symptoms first manifest themselves in motor skills and then in use of logic and reason. Many times (especially in the early stages), the individual with HD looks perfectly normal but will laugh at inappropriate times, drop things, stumble, and sometimes be accused of being drunk. However, the affected person doesn't recognize their own limitations and thinks that everything is just fine.

One time, my wife and I were blessed to win a trip to Hong Kong, and in our young lives, it was truly the trip of a lifetime! While in Hong Kong, naturally we wanted to tour, tour, tour, but I really became aware of how challenging it was to have a wife with physical and psychological issues, who was not even aware of those limitations. I had to be on guard every moment, kind of running interference for her as we would work our way through the crowded markets. We went on a guided tour one morning, and the guide advised everyone, "If you become separated from the group at any time, just make your way back to the bus and wait for us." At one point, we came upon a huge sprawling marketplace called the snake market. You guessed it; they sell snakes, small birds, and all the things that you need if you own a snake, like barrels filled with crickets, etc.… (I can't even begin to describe the smells in that place!) The crowd was particularly dense, and we followed our guide, who was holding up a small, red flag on a pole so we could see where he was at all times. Our group was pressing through into the snake market, and *suddenly* I lost my grip on Diana's hand… I looked quickly to my left, and there she was, wandering off quickly in another direction with a big smile on her face!

I was horrified and battled the crowd to try and get over to her but soon lost sight of her! "Dear Lord," I prayed, "keep your hand on Diana!" I separated from the tour group and decided that my best course of action would be to make my way back to the bus to wait for Diana. I waited for what seemed like *hours*, and suddenly there came Diana, weaving through the crowd, like a leaf blowing in the wind! I waved at her and darted over to take her hand, and she said, "I had an adventure!" I was so grateful to the Lord for his protection that day!

Something to think about:

Sometimes we take on more of the responsibility for our loved one's safety than God wants us to. God wants you to know that your loved one is truly in his hands and that he has a plan for their life. You are a big part of that plan. But just *know* that when you've done your part, you must trust God will do *his* part! Remember, God will not allow anyone who trusts in him to die until the work that God has planned for them has been accomplished. No one can change that. We need not fear dying because when we die, it's because our work on earth is completed, and God was ready to call us into his presence!

Let's pray:

Dear Lord, thank you for your protection and provision we take so much for granted in our lives! As we do our part to fulfill your plan for our lives, help us to turn our cares and burdens over to you! First Peter 5:7 says, "Cast all your anxiety on him because he cares for us." You've given us permission to let you carry our burdens, Lord, so I am casting my cares on you right now. *Amen*!

Chapter 22

Whatever Things Are Good, Think on Those Things!

My mother was such an amazing woman, an example of how to live life well and truly to the fullest. As she aged, she made adjustments and more adjustments, based on her physical ability. She loved to do needlework, so she had made many projects of embroidery and cross-stitch. But soon she found that it was just too hard for her to see. Finally, as her last needlework project, she struggled through a crewel embroidery picture of a lion, which she gave to my little son. We cherish that to this day! She loved reading her Bible. But the type was getting too small, so she switched to a large-type version and eventually to listening to Bible teaching on television.

Many of us fight against changes. And while some of those changes should be resisted, there are many that are simply a part of life. One area of change is aging. Even when we have stayed in pretty good physical condition, as we age, we find that it takes longer to heal from an injury, especially broken bones. One day, my mother was recovering from a pretty serious ankle injury and decided that she could walk across the room in her home using a walker. Well, she took a few steps and fell and caused even more injury and great pain! Her injuries were significant enough that it was decided it would be necessary for her to stay in a recovery center until she regained as much mobility as possible.

Upon arriving at the recovery facility, her room was assigned, and my sister, Kathy, wheeled her down the hall in her wheelchair to the room where she would be staying. The room light was not on, so there was only a tiny light coming from the single window. The room was a typical care facility room, pastel painted walls, tile floor, and sparse furnishings. Upon entering the room, my mother exclaimed, "Oh, it's lovely!" My sister was startled because she knew that my mother's vision was very diminished, and she had a hard time seeing anything more than basic shapes and colors and only when there was sufficient light. My sister said, "Mom, can you see the room? The light's not even on yet!" My mother smiled and said, "Well, I don't need to actually see it because I choose to believe it's lovely!"

Something to think about:
Many times, we are not able to alter our circumstances, so it's up to us to *decide* to look on the bright side. *Happiness* depends on your situation and circumstances, but *true joy* lives within and is not

determined by outside influences. God is the true joy giver, comforter, deliverer, and friend that sticks closer than a brother. Make sure, when you are feeling overwhelmed to cry out to God, ask him to restore your joy in spite of the turmoil that may be around you.

Let's pray:

Lord, your Word says that you will renew my strength, allowing me to rise up on wings as eagles (Isaiah 40:31). Father, I'm not feeling that right now. I'm discouraged, beaten down, and weary. I pray that you will forgive my doubt and renew my strength. Give me rest in my body and my spirit so that I will have true joy! Your mercies are new every morning, Father! Great is thy faithfulness (Lamentations 3:23–23). *Amen.*

Chapter 23

The Best Revenge

There are so many quotes and stories about people getting their revenge on those who have wronged them or about unfair situations; about illness that kept them from getting promoted in their job; or because someone kept them from completing their degree, and they never had time to go to college. Perhaps you decided, the only way to provide for your family was to take a job working halfway across the world from them for long periods of time, and during those times, your kids were growing up, and your spouse was lonely too. You felt so trapped and that life in general has wronged you.

There are Chinese proverbs, and even *Aesop's Fables* that deal with revenge. Everything seems to point to what a rich, sweet feeling it is to finally obtain that revenge!

Know what? Our Father knows that you are giving up so many things in order to care for your loved one. Maybe you've had to leave that great position at work, or perhaps that very special vacation has become impossible now. God's word speaks to this subject, from *front to back*!

One thing is clear; God sees your service and understands your sense of loss. God is *good*. Whatever you have given up in this life, in service to him and to others, will be repaid to you abundantly!

Romans 12:19 says, "Do not take revenge, my dear friends, but leave room for God's wrath, for it is written: 'It is mine to avenge; I will repay,' says the Lord."

Psalms 23:5 says, "You prepare a table before me in the presence of my enemies. You anoint my head with oil; my cup overflows."

John 10:10 says, "The thief comes only to steal, kill, and destroy, but I have come that you might have *life* more abundantly."

Something to think about:

The best way to remove the sadness and sense of disappointment that sometimes tries to overwhelm your thoughts is to do as Philippians 4:8 tells us: "Finally, brothers and sisters, whatever is true, whatever is noble, whatever is right, whatever is pure, whatever is lovely, whatever is admirable—if anything is excellent or praiseworthy—think about such things." God's Word also says that for a spirit of heaviness, the best solution is praise and worship (Isaiah 61:3). If you lift up your voice to God and praise him, you'll begin to feel release from burdens! Even if this is not something that you have ever done in your life, you should give it a try! Get alone somewhere, maybe even in your car as you're driving, and simply tell God that you recognize he is great and that he is the Lord of all creation! If you do that from a sincere heart, you will be astonished at the sense of well-being that begins to flow into your body!

Let's pray:

Lord, we know that there is one who seeks to destroy us emotionally and in every other way. He instills thoughts of anger and hurt and tries to make us feel as though we are victims at the hands of others. Father God, I am coming to you to ask that you give me a desire to release the people who have harmed me and to forgive them. Help me to fill my mind with thoughts of joy and of all the good things that you have provided in my life. Remind me of your great mercies and provision shown to me so often! Keep me close to you, Father! *Amen!*

Chapter 24

A Year of Firsts

During the first year after my wife died, some of the most-challenging things to experience were the "*first time without Diana*" events. She passed away midyear. So when Halloween rolled around, there I was at the door, greeting kiddos and handing out candy, but…for the first time in nearly five decades, Diana was not by my side, then came the Thanksgiving feast with all the family, and I didn't set a place for Diana at the table. Christmas came, and well, no Christmas presents needed to be bought for her. It's hard to express the impact that each of these *firsts* had on me. I would sit quietly and try to remember her smile when the kids came to the door, her joy when decorating for Christmas…

I still have those memories and still have an empty place in my heart. I ask God, "Father, when will my heart heal and not feel this loss?" It seems that the answer is, we learn to capture new memories, new happiness, and new experiences to balance the feelings of loss. I'm confident I'll never stop loving Diana, but I must admit it's far different now. A treasure I keep down in my heart that is not visible to others, something very private I can now cherish!

Something to think about:

My wife has been gone for some years now, and the old saying, "life goes on," appears to be true. I was told, "Just give it time" and "It will get easier with time" and "Time heals." There is some truth to these sayings. One thing is for sure, it's the memories of time spent together, travels together, laughter and tickling and teasing together...those are the things that remain, things you bought, things you owned, houses you had, fancy cars you had... none of those things matter as time goes on. This proves that we must focus on the eternal, the things that actually matter!

Let's pray:

Dear Lord, thank you for bringing me through this difficult season of my life. Please continue to heal my heart, Father. Restore my joy, and help me to have a heart full of thankfulness for all you've done for me! Let me be an encouragement to others. Use me in your eternal plan, Father! Help me to create new memories filled with happiness, friendships, and love! *Amen*!

Chapter 25

It's All about Balance

With Huntington's disease, as well as many other disorders, the affected person suffers from loss of balance, loss of equilibrium, and is sometimes disoriented, which causes them to be very unsteady. Over the years, as Diana's HD progressed, initially she was just unsteady in situations, like stairs and ramps, stepping off of curbs, and so on. Then came a stage where she could walk with some assistance but only so long as she was moving forward. Once she stopped or tried to stand still, she would tend to fall over! We developed ways to compensate, so she didn't have to feel quite as self-conscious. For example, when we were in church, the pastor would ask us to stand when praying, or sometimes the song leader would ask us to stand. We had a neat little trick! I would be on her left. And as we stood up, I'd slip my arm around her waist and position my right leg behind her left leg so that she could lean against me without appearing to do so. We developed lots of little tricks like that, and it's part of our story.

The most important balance we need to achieve in our lives is not associated with physically balancing ourselves; instead it's about balancing our emotions and our *thought lives*. No matter how exhausted we become, how overwhelmed we might feel, we must take care of ourselves. Make it a priority to spend time in prayer, reading the Bible, reading a favorite book, watching the cooking channel, or whatever gives you that escape from your challenging caregiving responsibilities. Sometimes this involves getting help from a friend or family member. My precious niece, Rhoda, came every Saturday for several years to help me by preparing an entire week's supply of the processed foods needed to be able to feed Diana. There were several years where I literally didn't want to live. I was so overwhelmed from the unrelenting requirements of caregiving, job, and personal health. I finally asked for help and honestly owe my life to my nephew, Troy, who selflessly sat with my wife several days a week from 7:00 p.m. until midnight so I could sleep for a few hours!

Something to think about:

The bottom line is, you cannot do it alone. Oh, you might be very strong, talented, and have the skills needed for your caregiving duties, but you do not have the emotional or mental strength you *think* you do. Almost anyone can handle a challenging care situation for a while. But if you are in it for the long haul, *get help*. Reach out first to the Lord, and spend time in prayer regularly because he is the true joy giver. Next, find a friend or family member who can give you breaks. It might only be long enough for you to go sit at a coffee shop for an hour, but it can be life-changing.

Let's pray:

Dear Heavenly Father, help us to balance our lives as we strive to live, as you would have us do. I pray your Holy Spirit will bring peace to me and fill me with a joy only you can bring. Lord, I know that when I'm feeling defeated and exhausted, the enemy of my soul can cause me to doubt your love and care for me, and I pray that you will give me wisdom to recognize that when those thoughts come, they are not from you! In your Word, you've told us in Psalm 103:1–2, "Praise the Lord, my soul; all my inmost being, praise his holy name. Praise the Lord, my soul, and forget not all his benefits!" *Amen*!

Chapter 26

The Power of Words

A few years ago, during a family get-together at our home in Omaha, I was pleased to have so many members of our extended family attend. Some, like my brother-in-law, Jim, drove for many hours to be a part of the gathering. I've always admired him. When he married my oldest sister, I was only four years old and was the ring bearer at their wedding! As I grew up, he was always a part of my life, teaching me things, both by his words and by his actions. (You can tell I admired this man greatly!) We were sitting around a table, visiting, and he was asking me about the business I'd started, how I did it, what the challenges were, etc., and he told me that what I'd accomplished was impressive. This really humbled me, as this man had accomplished so *much* in his life! He had founded a number of successful businesses, operated large farms, and even mined gold in South America! I responded by saying, "Well, thank you, Jim. It's true that God has really blessed me, and I'm very grateful!" He paused and said, "Yes, he has blessed you. However, you are an extraordinary individual." I was so taken aback that I was almost speechless! This man did not suffer fools and never handed out insincere compliments. He reserved his admiration for very, very few.

I have cherished that conversation every day since then, and I can still hear his voice in my head, saying, "However, you are an extraordinary individual."

Something to think about:

Never underestimate the power of your words. Caregivers tend to have periods where the burdens they carry cause them to turn inward and focus on the continual requirements of their duties for their loved one. Stop right now, take a deep breath, and consider what you might do or say to the person you're caring for that will help them with the emotional struggle with which they are dealing. At your toughest moments, you will be astonished to find that when you reach outward and speak *life* into the spirit of the one for which you are providing care, then even *your* burden becomes lighter as well.

You never know where anyone is in their daily walk. They may be on top of the world, or they may be in a true struggle about which others are unaware. People with whom you come into contact are hungry for a kind word, a word of encouragement or a thoughtful comment. They will spot a phony instantly, so your words must be sincere. You don't need some monumental accomplishment in order to have that kind interaction; sometimes it might be simply, "Hey, I'm really happy to see you!" or "I want you to know that I've been thinking about you and praying for you!"

Let's pray:

Father, please let me see others through your eyes. Let me have a heart for others! Please give me opportunities to bless others today with encounters that you arrange. Let me be your arms extended. Let me be a resource to my spouse, my children, my friends, to the servers at the restaurant, the checkout person at the store… They all have burdens that my encouraging words might help to lighten! I'll give *you* the glory, Lord! Amen!

Chapter 27

The Midnight Hour

Diana was ill. She was battling some sort of bad cold/flu. If you or I have the flu, it's miserable. If someone with Huntington's has the flu, it's dangerous and life-threatening. Individuals with HD cannot self-stimulate helpful actions, like blowing their nose or clearing their throat. Instead, mucus and fluids build up and flow, and caregivers must be vigilant. If it builds up too much, there is danger of mucus or infectious particles entering their lungs, which is very dangerous.

In this type of situation, it's hard *not* to think of all the worrisome information you've read. I read that 54 percent of deaths of HD patients are caused by pneumonia—most notably, aspiration pneumonia (the kind caused by food or water in the lungs). I also read that the median survival of Huntington's disease is fifteen to eighteen years after onset of symptoms. The average age of death for a person with HD is fifty-four to fifty-five years of age. Diana was sixty-two, and her onset of symptoms was thirty-two years prior, so, *yea, Diana*, and praise the Lord! She was a fighter.

We held hands. She listened intently as I prayed for her, and we both had a renewed sense of how precious and fleeting life can be.

Diana was breathing a little better after a few hours. She was sitting up in her wheelchair, as lying down was out of the question with the danger of aspiration. We spent the rest of the night holding hands and just being together. Oh, how I wished that she could have shared her thoughts with me during the scary and challenging time! We could only look into one another's eyes as I whispered encouragement and prayed.

Something to think about:

Recognize that we are all only a heartbeat away from eternity. Don't dwell on the *"what if"* or the *"what will I do if"* thoughts that will inevitably arise. Cherish each moment with your loved one. Turn off the TV and talk. Put your phone away, and don't surf the Internet. Dedicate time to true communication with your loved one and with God.

Let's pray:

Father God, thank you for your care, your provision, and for friends and our families who care. Thank you, Lord, for giving Diana strength and allowing her to eventually breathe more fully that night. You knew that it was not her time to come home to heaven. You still had work for her to do. You knew that Diana would be a testimony for your goodness and provision, even when she could not speak. Her life was an ongoing testimony to you, Father! God, we recognize and affirm that you know how to care for what belongs to you! *Amen!*

Chapter 28

Change, Change, and More Change

Here's something that everyone already knows, but we all have a natural tendency to stubbornly resist. That's right, it's the dreaded word *change*! Change usually means uncertainty and loss of control. We typically avoid change so that we can remain comfortable in our status quo. Couples who are together for a long time find that they undergo many changes—changes in where they live, changes in careers, changes involving children, changes in health, moving to new homes, and more! There is an area of our lives where the changes are going to require us to adapt in order to be successful in our relationships. My wife and I were married for forty-seven years. And believe me, we were not the same people at forty that we were at twenty, nor were we the same people at sixty that we were at forty! People often remarked that we were "lucky that we both changed along the same ways." But honestly, it's so much *more* than luck!

Your happiness and well-being in life are determined almost completely by your attitude regarding the inevitable changes that will most certainly come. I learned so much from my wife's attitude! Early in our married life, my career required many relocations throughout the country in order to advance in my profession. We moved seventeen times in the first twenty-one years of our marriage. And when I would tell my wife the news that I'd been offered a promotion, but we would need to move to another city, she looked upon it as an adventure! When I told her that we were moving to Salt Lake City from Wichita, she said, "Okay, I'll get to ski!" And when I told her we were moving from Atlanta to Tampa, she said, "Okay, I get to lay on a beach!" (*I owe her so much!*)

The real facts of each move were very hard. She had to move away from friends. She had to leave the church that she had grown to love. She had to leave a home that she had just finished decorating. Sometimes it meant moving far away from my family. But in almost every instance, it was the fact that she *decided* to be happy that allowed her to continue in a joyful state of mind. Her mood was never dependent upon something wonderful happening; it was because she *decided* to be happy and had committed the matter to the Lord, in whom she had complete confidence.

Something to think about:

There is much to be said about how to be happy in life. One thing that is really useful is to carefully watch the lives of people who exhibit a lot of joy and seem to be enjoying their lives. What is their secret? If they are honest with you, they would tell you that their lives are filled with adversity, just like yours, but they have simply *chosen* to be happy and to do fulfilling things, which then cause the internal joy to grow. These people are individuals who add value to everything and everyone through their giving, their acts of service, and the constant kindnesses, which they demonstrate daily. Buy someone's coffee. Tell someone that they have a beautiful smile. Recognize someone's accomplishments. One of the activities that gave my wife joy was to send greeting cards. She sent Christmas cards, Easter cards, birthday cards. She even sent St. Patrick's Day cards! She could easily picture the smile on their faces when they opened her cards!

Let's pray:

Father, please help me to accept the changes that come in my life and to face them with joy! In your Word, you've shown us over and over that *you* are the true joy giver, so I ask that you fill my heart with joy. Lord, also give me inspiration about how I can add value to the lives of others. Help me develop the heart of a servant. Bless me as I learn to bless others and to view changes as opportunities to serve you through my service to others! Amen!

Chapter 29

The Little Things Are the Big Things

If someone were to ask you to list the most important things from your entire lifetime, you would tend to prioritize big life events, huge milestones, and significant career achievements. But as we get older and can really reflect on our lives, the things that hold tender spots in our hearts and minds are different from the big achievements or milestones. Instead, we discover that many little things were truly the big things; the memorable things, the endearing things. These are the things that actually define quality of life for you and for your loved one. As my wife's health declined, the things that made her smile and were meaningful to her were when I would bring her a chai tea latte, a Mylar balloon, or some flowers. Those things meant more to her than when I bought her a sapphire necklace. My sweet mother, even at one hundred years old, simply loved hard candies to suck on. She might not have asked for them, but when we would give her some, she would laugh in delight!

You have to ask yourself, What are the "little things" that are important to my loved one? My wife loved roses, swans, little mouse figurines, and clothing in her favorite color of blue. There could come a time when your loved one is no longer able to express their thoughts well, so it's important for you to know their love languages. It may sound too silly, but…start making a list. Each time you remember something that is really special to your wife, your husband, your parents, etc.…add it to the list. Make it an ongoing list, always evolving and growing. You'll be very happy you've made this effort! Be ready to fulfill the fun little things that they might not be able to ask for. Make sure that you know their favorite candy bar, what kind of tea they prefer, and as many other small things as possible so that you can bring joy to them later when these small things will be incredibly meaningful.

Something to think about:

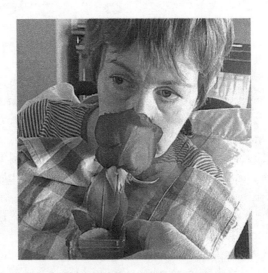

It's too bad that most of us don't learn early in life how to recognize the most important things and prioritize them! Our lives are so full and busy that days, weeks, months, and then years fly by, and we have focused on certain career goals, bigger houses, and temporal things instead of understanding that the meaningful, lasting things are usually not the big things but a collection of little things that add up to wonderful, lasting relationships and memories. It's surprising to find out how few of us actually know the *three most important priorities* of our wives or husbands or others who are so important in our lives. You might think you know, but I would challenge you to sit down together and do this little exercise: Your wife or husband is to write down their top three most important priorities currently. You then are to write down what you believe their top three priorities are. Then compare the lists! (Naturally, I used the "husband and wife" example, but apply this idea to all of your important relationships!)

Let's pray:

Lord, you know our hearts, our thoughts, and our dreams. You've said in your Word that you will give us the desires of our hearts. But we know that first we must make sure that our desires are in agreement with your plans for our lives. Help us to know how to serve you by serving others! Help us to be intentional about knowing the little things in the lives of those around us so we can bless them and create more meaningful relationships, which will stand the test of time and last through eternity! *Amen!*

Chapter 30

Cherish the Moments

I had a very sobering moment one night in 2016, about 9:30 p.m. We were watching TV, and suddenly, I became aware of unusual movements from Diana. I looked over at her, and she was choking. Her face was white, her eyes wide, and she was reaching out into the air with her arms. I rushed to her and quickly checked her mouth to ensure there was nothing lodged there that I didn't know about; it was clear. She literally couldn't get a single gasp of air. It was her own saliva, somehow down the airway, which was causing the blockage! I prayed as I lifted her arms high to open her airways… It didn't help. My sister, Kathy, was in the other room, and I heard her say, "This is real, isn't it!" (She was scared!) I decided to get the special device we have to assist with clearing airways (suction tube). But the moment I took a step toward the counter to get it (I keep it handy!), she suddenly sputtered and gasped and began to gulp in air.

I hugged her and prayed with her. I asked her if she was scared, and she said an emphatic "uh huh!" I spent a long while just hugging her and assuring her that God had his hand on her and that I was here for her. She held my hands tightly and wouldn't let go. After a while, we went to bed, but I was bothered by a gurgling, rasping sound as she breathed, liquid still in her deep airway. Not good. This could quickly lead to aspiration (leading cause of death in HD patients). We prayed and prayed… Suddenly, she coughed several times, and it cleared! (Praise the Lord!)

This was different from the many times daily that Diana struggled with food and choked a little, etc.… This had been *the real deal*. The realization washed over me that this could have been *it*. In a couple of minutes, I could have lost her. I'm so glad Diana was in the palm of his loving hands and that she knew the Lord. So someday, when that day came, she would pass into a wonderful, Huntington's-free body with eternal life and joy.

Something to think about:

Our days are filled with appointments, doctor's visits, meal preparation, or perhaps helping our loved one with feeding or bathing. Hours pass, another night, another day, another week, and suddenly we realize it's a month later. It is so important to be *totally intentional* about creating memories with your loved one that will last. Tasks we do are necessary, but they will not become the memories we cherish later. Surprise your loved one with something out of the ordinary, not expected, that will create a moment of joy for both of you to remember. If you don't plan to do these things, time will slip by, and you'll have missed another chance for a blessing and a memory.

Let's pray:

Father, you were *intentional* in demonstrating your love for each of us throughout all time. You were intentional when you said, "It is not good for man to be alone." You were intentional when you created a way for mankind to have a personal relationship with you through your Son. Help me to plan to do good things for my loved one and for those around me each day. Help my mind to dwell on how to create blessings and memories to cherish. Amen!

Chapter 31

Can I Endure This Hardship?

When the challenges in our lives are seemingly overwhelming, and we are at wit's end, and we are physically, mentally, and emotionally exhausted, it's time to take a step back and pray for God's grace in our situation. People often misquote the Bible verse 1 Corinthians 10:13 and say, "Don't worry, God won't give you more than you can bear." What the verse *actually* says is that God won't allow you to be tempted beyond what you can bear but will provide a way to escape the temptation. The myth that God won't let you have too much hardship is just not in the Bible! In fact, in 2 Corinthians 1:8–11, Paul told us that he himself was under terrible pressure, *beyond his ability to endure*. He actually felt as though he had received a sentence of death. He went on to explain then that his situation was so that he would learn not to rely on himself but on God.

Something to think about:

Here are some points to remember when you're facing terrible pressure, depression, or fatigue:

1. God may not take away your difficulty, but he has promised to be with you through it. He will be beside you, listen to you, comfort you, and guide you.
2. God is good. This is hard to internalize when you're facing such terrible challenges, but it's true. He cares for you, and he cares about you. He knows you personally because he created you. Lean on him.
3. You're in this situation for a reason. God is building your character, testing you to see if you will be faithful. Believe me, you're no Job (from the Bible), but God does take pleasure when his children honor him with their attitudes and trust. Ask God to open your spiritual eyes to show you what he wants you to learn from this hardship.
4. After you've come through this challenging season of your life, *use* the experiences and learnings you've received to bless and help others that are facing hardship. God will honor your service!

Let's pray:

Father, please help me to trust you completely with my life and the life of my loved one. Forgive me for trying to rely on my own strength because I know that I can't handle all these things alone. Lord, you are my provider, my healer, my protector, and the one who loved me before I ever even knew you. Help me to rest in you, to allow your Holy Spirit to minister to me. Give me wisdom for each day! Amen!

Diana's Graduation

As always, I woke at 5:00 a.m. and quietly snuck out of bed, careful not to disturb Diana. I made sure she was okay and slipped out of the room to prepare her medications for later, when our helper would arrive. I went to my home office to check mail while listening to Diana's breathing through the monitor I keep at my desk. At about 6:00 a.m., her breathing sounded labored, so I decided to go in and see if she was too hot. I pulled off a cover, and sure enough, she was hot, and removing the cover gave her some relief. I went back to my office, and at about 6:30 a.m., I noticed that I could not hear her breathing via the monitor. That wasn't so unusual, as sometimes she would roll over and face away from her monitor, so I didn't think too much about it. At 7:30 a.m., I went up to do the next part of preparations: select her clothes for the day and lay them out. Diana seemed to be sleeping *very* soundly.

At 8:00, her sweet helper arrived, and we would always enjoy going into the bedroom together and say, "Good morning, Diana," and get her day started. Diana was still sleeping, it seemed. I told our helper to go ahead and change Diana and bathe her. And if she wanted to sleep, let her, and I would come up when it was time to lift her into her wheelchair.

My niece, Rhoda, arrived at 8:30 to work in my little business and looked in on the helper who was with Diana. She came to me and said, "Phil, something is wrong. You need to come upstairs now!" I rushed up the stairs and into the room, where the helper was very upset but remaining as calm as possible. I checked for pulse, checked for breathing…could not detect anything. I told them, "I will get Diana into the van and to the emergency room faster than any ambulance could get here, so help me get her into the chair."

I knew, as I was wheeling her to the van, that she was gone…but rushed off to the hospital anyway, praying and weeping as I drove. Upon arriving at the emergency room, I shouted, "Unresponsive," as I wheeled her in, and the medical team leapt into action, taking her quickly to a prep room. They began CPR and asked if she had a living will, and I let them know that she was "DNR" (do not resuscitate), and they stopped the CPR at once. Some tests were run, and she was declared dead upon arrival. I believe that she died at 6:30 a.m. when I could no longer hear her breathing…and the doctors agreed that would be about right, based on their observations.

The two hardest things I can ever remember doing in my entire life were when I finally walked out of that room, knowing that was the last time I would see her earthly body, and then when I pushed that empty wheelchair back up into the handicap van.

Something to think about:

There is no way to fully prepare yourself for the death of a loved one. You just visited with Dad yesterday, and today you get *the call*… He's gone. Grandma was doing so well, but today her heart failed suddenly. Even when your loved one had an extended illness that "everyone knew" was terminal, the actual event comes upon you like an enveloping cloud, a numbness that is hard to fight your way through.

You walk back into your home, and all the everyday things lying around suddenly scream a memory back into your mind. Her sweater draped over a chair, the medicines in their little amber bottles, and all that medical equipment.

"Move on" sounds so trite at a time like this, but getting things like medicines and medical equipment out of your everyday view will help your heart at that time. I'm so thankful to my sister and my wife's sisters who removed my wife's clothes from the closet and helped me through that job!

The most important step you can take is to take some of the newfound time to draw close to God. Spend intentional time worshipping and seeking his face in prayer. Even if you think you don't know how, just reach out to Jesus and ask him to be the leader of your life right then and there, and he will give you peace.

Let's pray:

Father God, your Word is filled with promises of comfort and help, and we claim these promises for our reader today! You've promised that you will draw near to the brokenhearted and that you would be with us during times of trouble! You'll never leave us or forsake us. You'll be a friend that sticks closer than a brother! You'll be our provider, and Jesus has even called us friend! Help us to listen for your voice, Lord! Amen.

Epilogue

At 6:30 *a.m.*, on Monday, August 19, 2019, Diana was awakened by a gentle hand on her shoulder. She opened her eyes in awe as she realized *everything* was different, everything was clear, her body no longer was bound by Huntington's disease! Instantly, she realized the hand on her shoulder belonged to the one she has waited her entire life to see. Jesus looked into her eyes and, laughing joyfully, said, "Diana, *well done*! You have been so faithful! Come with me, and let me show you everything I've prepared for you!" She took his hand. And in the distance, she heard the cheering and excited voices of scores of loved ones: her mom and daddy, JoAnn, Luanna, Dad and Mom Leichliter, and dozens more people who she knew were waiting for her because they had put their faith in Christ long ago! Behind them were thousands upon thousands of angels, more beautiful than she could imagine, all cheering and beaconing her!

Joy. Laughter. Delight. And look…the throne of the Father!

At 6:30 a.m., on Monday August 19, 2019, someone else also awoke in a start. A horrible sense of dread and fear gripped him as he desperately looked about the room, trying to understand what was happening. Off in the distance, he saw Jesus walking away with Diana, the heavenly host cheering. Instantly, the realization of what was happening swept over him. He shouted, "Jesus, wait for me! Wait for me!" Jesus looked back over his shoulder and said sadly, "Depart from me. I never knew you…" Suddenly, cold hands gripped his arms and legs and began to drag him backward, *away* from the joy, the laughter, the delight, toward utter darkness where he could hear wailing and crying, separation from Christ for eternity, entering into a place that was not even prepared for him but for those fallen angels who rebelled against God. But because he rejected Christ during his life, he would be entering this horrible place too…

Something to think about:

Every…single…one of us will have *one* of these two experiences. *None* of us gets out of this thing alive. If you're reading this, you will be making a choice right now. *Which* experience will you have when your time comes? Every individual on earth must answer the question, "What am I going to do with Christ Jesus?"

Let's pray:

Father God, I pray that you will make yourself very real to the reader just now and that if they have not asked Jesus into their heart, to be the leader of their life, they will do that right now. Just a simple prayer: "God, I know I've sinned. I know that I'm not able to live up to your standards without Jesus in my life. Jesus, please come into my heart. I want to make you the leader of my life. Amen!"

Words of wisdom from Andrea Zanko, MS, genetic counselor, University of California at San Francisco, Genetics Clinic; retired and creator of the UCSF Huntington's Disease Clinic:

I am here to offer a reminder that the *caregiver* must also be open to *receiving care*. The following paragraphs are to encourage you not to withdraw, not to disappear. In addition to educating yourself about resources and keeping things sweet and simple and safe, there are foundational tips to face each day with balance, compassion, patience, and love.

You matter. Do not lose yourself while caring for your loved one. Be a witness to your own needs. The following thoughts are encouraged to be in concert—i.e., these ideas are interrelated and can benefit from a multisystem approach.

Pay attention to your emotional changes. Recognizing and accurately naming your feelings can be powerful. Are you sad, or are you angry? Are you frightened, or are you frustrated? By sorting out the source of your feelings, you can begin to address them appropriately. And this is often not an *or* situation but an *and* situation. It is certainly possible to feel love and anger at the same time. It is possible to hold sadness and joy together. Your situation is personal, unique, your own. You may have emotional swings by the week or the hour or from moment to moment. Pause. Breathe. Move to music. Reach out. It is normal.

Your spiritual needs are likely very personal. Caregiving is the most loving, kind, thoughtful experience, *and* it may be the most challenging. Time limitation may not allow you to connect with your religious community as you had before. Your values may be disrupted; your faith may be questioned. Why? Why my loved one? However, wherever you find peace and support, remember, there is no judgment, *and* it is never too late to seek the love and guidance and support and strength from your personal spiritual source. It may be a walk in the woods…listening to a healing chant…meditating or doing yoga…reading a psalm or poem. Those moments for your revitalization are critical for your well-being. If your loved one can attend your place of worship, continue to do so as that sense of belonging is just as nurturing for you as for him/her.

This brings us to your social world. Your loved one is your world, understood, but you cannot do this alone. Without community—friends, family members, congregation—you can disappear. There is no question about your love; that is not the issue. You grow and flourish with the support and love of others. They want to be part of your life and may not know how best to do so. What to say…what to do…they miss you and your loved one! The longer and higher you build that fence, the more space between. Communicate with your community. Honestly let them know how they can help or how meaningful it would be to simply be present. *You matter.* Yes, I am repeating those words because you are so busy caring for another; you forget how nice it is to have a dialogue about something else. You might forget how nice a smile from a friend makes you feel. You might forget that sharing a joke or listening to music with friends can still happen. And when it does, it can encourage you to cope better, not feel alone, and ultimately be a more present caregiver.

Finally, let's look at your physical needs. Your well-being depends on maintaining activities that you are well aware of. No one needs to tell you the importance of sleep, good nutrition, exercise, and relaxation. As the caregiver, your hours are probably erratic, and your diet may be quick and easy. Exercise may be lifting and dressing and bathing....and relaxation may be nonexistent. But you matter. This is when respite, even for one hour, can allow you time to replenish. This may be a long commitment; the duration is likely simply unknown.

There are books and songs and poems about the amazement of not knowing. Moment by moment, your loved one may experience unanticipated changes. Remember that all is transient. Forget linear reasoning, and try to embrace resilience and flexibility. More is being asked of you with less time for nourishing your soul. And then your loved one smiles, and you are struck with a moment of awe and gratitude—gratitude for that moment.

About the Author

Phil Leichliter lives in Tennessee, although his work career allowed him and his family to live in many cities around the United States. He spent most of his career in retail, starting very early in life, selling candy to neighborhood children and eventually working as an executive with a large Fortune 500 company based in California.

When his wife, Diana, was diagnosed with Huntington's disease, he determined that he would be the one to give her care and provide her with the comfort of staying in her own home. Very soon it became apparent that he would need to be with her 24-7 for her safety and care, so he had to develop a way to work from home. (But…that's another story!)

Phil doesn't define himself as a *retailer*; he instead preferred to define himself first as a dedicated follower of Jesus Christ, then a husband, a father, and a caregiver. That role as caregiver gave him a wealth of experience, which he has always sought to share with others who might find themselves in a caregiver role. He realized that by sharing his experiences and thoughts with others, he might fulfill God's calling on his life to encourage caregivers and give hope to those who find themselves challenged and perhaps overwhelmed by the enormity of the responsibilities of their everyday lives as caregivers.

We hope you will enjoy his stories and share them with others!

Printed in the USA
CPSIA information can be obtained
at www.ICGtesting.com
CBHW032104161124
17547CB00010B/429